LETTERS FROM A FOLLOWER, CHARU GUPTA, TO THE LEADER, 'MR. RAHUL GANDHI'.

CHARU GUPTA

Copyright © Charu Gupta
All Rights Reserved.

This book has been published with all efforts taken to make the material error-free after the consent of the author. However, the author and the publisher do not assume and hereby disclaim any liability to any party for any loss, damage, or disruption caused by errors or omissions, whether such errors or omissions result from negligence, accident, or any other cause.

While every effort has been made to avoid any mistake or omission, this publication is being sold on the condition and understanding that neither the author nor the publishers or printers would be liable in any manner to any person by reason of any mistake or omission in this publication or for any action taken or omitted to be taken or advice rendered or accepted on the basis of this work. For any defect in printing or binding the publishers will be liable only to replace the defective copy by another copy of this work then available.

This book is dedicated to my father, Mr. Pradeep Kumar Gupta, who has always inspired me to be fearless and intelligent.

Contents

Foreword

This book is essentially for those who desire a change in politics and for those who seek honesty in this system.

Acknowledgements

I am thankful to the congress party and its leaders who are always willing and interested to listen to the new voices aspiring to be future leaders.

CHAPTER ONE

LETTERS

Letters from a follower (Charu Gupta) to the leader (Mr. Rahul Gandhi)

Presented below are few of the letters written by me to my leader Sh. Rahul Gandhiji. The letters include the date on which they were written. This collection of letters include my ideas, suggestions and some ideas for manifesto promise for the congress party. Some of them have also been sent to the government of India as suggestions from a vigilant citizen.

1. Aspirations of a congressi

27th June 2020

Sir,

Current political scene affecting the social scene

We need to change the track of the governance to the right direction of development and progress. We must inculcate the confidence in the public that congress party leaders are there with them in their time of need and will continue to make policies for their welfare in future also. They shouldn't be fearful of the opponent party in raising their voice. Its not the voice of dissent its their constitutional right to raise their voice against any discrimination and participate in the process of democracy.

Ways and means to achieve the developed and progressed India

People's support and participation in the governance. Inclusion of new and daring leaders in the congress party. To continue to make policies for the welfare of the people for contemporary problems.

Vision for the future of India

A self reliant, developed and competitive India in all the fields. To be able to give to the people of India all the necessary amenities irrespective of their financial conditions. To give them a fearless atmosphere to grow and develop.

Contribution of the congress parties old leaders and expectations from the young leaders

Congress party's contribution has been selfless till the present date in the growth and development of India. From the establishing of big industries, dams, to green revolution, nationalization of banks, to the computerisation to the exemplary laws like MGNREGA, RTI, RTF, RTE, anganwadi schemes, work done in the sector of primary education. We expect our young leaders to be equally contributing and intelligent.

Dreams for the future of India

A developed, peaceful, prosperous and fearless india.

Steps to achieve the above-mentioned aim

To make congress win by informing the people about the above-mentioned points and to inform the public about the future welfare schemes of the congress.

2. Influences in a man's life

26th september 2020

Sir,

There are three big influences in a man's life - God, Parents and the government. God for providing us every necessity in plenty for the survival of this human body i.e. food, air and water. Parents for giving us birth and enabling us to witness this wonderful world and giving us all means necessary for our nourishment. Govt. for providing us all the remaining necessities and services for making our life easy. Money is a commodity that a human is required to earn for his survival in the modern day world. To achieve that state of earning this is the duty of the government to provide them all the services and amenities. Previous congress governments and the congress party have played their role diligently in the service of the nation for the past 70 years. By enacting the laws like RTI for making the system transparent, RTF for providing food at subsidised rate to the 62% of the population, RTE for providing free and compulsory education to the children upto 14 years of age and programmes like anganwadi and mid day meals we have shown that we care for the well- being for the citizens of the India. Congress party has never indulged in supporting prejudice of any kind in the society. We want to ensure the public that we will continue to make laws, programmes and schemes for the development of India. Therefore, it is my sincere suggestion to the congress party to introduce 'The Basic Amenities Act' in its manifesto and circulate the idea in the Bihar elections. Under this Act Government of India will provide food, water, shelter, employment, education and health. The previous congress government under the leadership of Shri. Rahul Gandhi already accomplished half of this task. Congress party promises to do the rest of the task in the next tenure of its government. RTE, RTF and MGNREGA are the laws which have empowered the citizens of India. Remaining part is to achieve the task of providing employment, shelter, water and to strengthen the healthcare system and to make it more accessible to the public of India. Employment to the skilled and educated people of India can also be given by providing them a chance to be the entrepreneur and giving them land, money, infrastructure and machinery. to open up industries. Slowly and automatically they will become self-sufficient and come out of poverty. By keeping the ownership rights with itself the government will be able to earn the money for recurring expenditure of the scheme. This will also prevent brain drain from the country and encourage the children to make new and innovative technologies in India.

3. Be the change you wish to see

3rd October 2020

Sir,

If we the educated citizens of India want to bring about a change in the political system we must start by forming a correct, true and an honest opinion of the events happening around us. We should not let false misconceptions of the wrong individuals affect and influence us. We must continue to work towards improving the quality of our life by nurturing the thoughts that lead to the nourishment of mind and body. We must not hesitate to participate in the political process of democracy because we the people of India are the most important part of it. Our each vote matters. If there is something we want to change we must raise and take up the issue in the right and dignified manner with the right authority. We must continue to share our positive and encouraging thoughts with the fellow citizens with the intention to share the knowledge and the good feelings. We are the makers of our own destiny and responsible for the future of our country Therefore we should be positive and contributing towards the decisions for the actions to be taken in the interest of the country. I am proud to say that I am a 4th generation congressi from my family post independence and I will continue to contribute my ideas and suggestions for the betterment of the congress so that we all can see a bright future for the citizens of India.

4. Necessity of the 'Basic Amenities Act'

6th October 2020

Sir,

Intelligence is a virtue that is common in Indian children irrespective of their financial status. This quality of indian children is appreciated by leaders worldwide. The congress party promises to endow the children of India with all the amenities that will help them develop and enhance this quality of their personality in a fearless environment free from all the prejudices whether financial or based on any other bias. We promise to give them all the support necessary to help them grow as a nourished individual. That's why it is necessary to give their families all the support required for their mental and physical nourishment so that they can become the next generation luminaries in their field of excellence and are able to lead our country in all the competitions that are there in the world. We want to assure them that the congress party will fulfill the promise of giving them a prosperous future.

5. Expectations from and lessons for the children

8th October 2020

Sir,

1. Our parents expect us to lead a healthy, educated and a prosperous life. We are expected to pass on the moral teachings and the knowledge of leading a healthy lifestyle to our offspring to let them grow into a nourished individual to be able to make them a distinguished personality of a society where we are supposed to interact.

2. Our teachers expect us to get a correct knowledge of not only the subject taught but also the right attitude to face the competition that life offers and to be able to sustain the fight and come out as a winner. Academic excellence in India is related to the marks obtained in the school based on the excellence of knowledge in the subjects. But the real fight that life offers has to be won with the perseverance and the wisdom we gain through the experience as we move towards the win.

3. As the citizens of India we are expected to respect the heritage of India and to learn from the teachings thereby gained and continue to innovate in the direction of development and progress of our country. We should make our opinions about current affairs with an informed mind and should not have a discretion about any subject unrestricted by knowledge and correct information.

6. An empathetic message from a fellow congressi

18th October 2020

Sir,

1. We have full faith in our ability to lead our party to the victory and our country in the right direction of prosperity i.e. Developed India.

2. We will achieve our aim with full dedication and commitment as passed on to us by our early party leaders.

3. We are firm in our belief to achieve our objective of overall development of our country to achieve the desired result of an all-inclusive growth.

4. We are committed to remove all the prejudices which threaten the thoughts and affect the actions of the citizens of India.

5. We are dedicated to nurture the right kinds of thoughts and emotions in the citizens of India for an all-embracing progress of India.

6. Therefore, we request all the citizens of India to decide the next party to rule by using their judgement with utmost intelligence for the entire country's future depends upon their resolve to take our country in the right direction of evolution free from the clutches of all the abominations.

7. 'Basic Amenities Act' - Aim, Intention, objective, contribution

19th December 2020

Sir,

Written below are some of the relevant points related to the 'Basic Amenities Act', which is a suggestion given by me to the congress party to include in its policy paper for 2024 electrons and start engaging the public about the benefits of it.

'Basic Amenities Act' - Aim, Intention, objective, contribution

Aim

The act aims to provide six basic amenities viz. food, water, shelter, education, employment and health to all the needful citizens of India.

Intention

To provide for the progress and development of the people of our country.

objective

The objective of the enactment of the act is to provide nourishment both mental and physical to the people especially youth of the country which constitutes the major part of the population. The Act aims to lead our country on the path of human development and to make the citizens capable of sustaining a decent standard of living. As we desire to make our country a developed nation it is very important to work for the cause of human development and provide all the necessary amenities to the citizens which would enable them to attain a standard of living and dignified life and which would enable their future generations to thrive, bloom and flourish in a healthy environment.

Contribution

The act intends to contribute to the well being of the citizens and enhance their quality of life.

8. Role and contribution of congress party in the 70 years of its governance

21st December 2020

Sir,

Role and contribution of congress party in the 70 years of its governance

Right from the time of independence till today the Congress party has dedicated its work and efforts towards the sustenance of democracy and its ideals in India. We have developed a system of governance to achieve the above-mentioned task. Democracy means a system of governance which is of the people, by the people and for the people. We wholeheartedly believe in this principle and therefore, always dedicate our objectives and intentions in the fulfillment of the same. The system built by the congress party for the sustenance of democracy constitutes the entire process of governance and its machinery which includes all the ministries and the organizations, institutions and knowledge centres made thereunder. We have made utmost efforts to encourage freedom of expression, scientific temper, equality of opportunity, socialism, secularism and public participation in our style of governance because these are requisites in the functioning of a democracy to provide equal rights to all the citizens of India. We are committed to our aim of providing a bright and prosperous future to the children of India without any prejudice or bias. We want to thank all the Indian citizens for having faith in us and make a promise to them for the continuance of our efforts in the direction of a developed India.

9. The meaning of congress induced Prosperity in India

10th Feb 2021

Sir,

It is essential for an individual to think about prosperity. It is a necessity for the development of a country. In the present time, education is a prerequisite for an individual to attain prosperity. It makes us capable, intelligent, skilful and talented to achieve the desired status in the society. It helps us to achieve the desired status of development and progress for our country. Congress party promises to provide all the necessary opportunities and amenities to the citizens of India to attain that prosperity and necessary infrastructure to our country to be developed. We believe in the idea of educated, intelligent, developed and powerful India. We are dedicated to the attainment of the same. The laws made by our party under the leadership of Shri Rahul Gandhi ji are relevant and fruitful to attain the same. The consequence of the work done under the Congress-ruled government is the provision of the dignity of life to the citizens of India and the conclusion of which is a powerful, educated, self-sufficient and resultantly a developed India.

The consequence of the work done with hard work and intelligence and the correct strategy always results in the attainment of the victory of a great magnitude. in politics you can measure the success by the level and quantity of people agreeing with you. the success reflects in the common man's feelings towards the country and the love you can generate in their hearts for the fellow citizens. these parameters when obtained in great quantities and when mixed together will result in the alchemy that will be called as Developed and Prosperous India. the result of this development will last for a long time and the resultant effect will be prosperous and flourishing future generations. that's what a true leader wants. that's what Congress wants.

Our leader, Shri. Rahul Gandhiji, has tirelessly worked for the upliftment and welfare of the people of India. There is no iota of doubt about the intentions of our leader which is dedicated to the enhancement of the lives of the Indians.

The intelligence with which he executed the best of the laws, programmes and schemes in the interest of the nation is appreciable. His love, devotion and affection for the people of India is reflected in his work. Therefore, we want #RahulGandhiWalaIndia i.e. #CompassionateIndia.

#EducatedIndia

Our Leader believes in the power that education gives to the youth which gives strength to their mind and knowledge to their brain which further enables them to be successful in their life. Therefore, we want #RahulGandhiWalaIndia i.e. #EducatedIndia.

Our leader believes in the power that intelligence gives to the youth of India. Under his leadership, Congress party enacted 'RTE' Act. which aims to educate the children of India to facilitate the development of #IntelligentIndia.

The intelligence acquired through education will enable them to achieve the prosperity they desire for themselves and for our country. Therefore, we want #RahulGandhiWalaIndia i.e. #IntelligentIndia.

Real power is in the cumulative prosperity and strength of the people of a country. Our leader has worked whole-heartedly to make all the citizens of India powerful.

Under his leadership Congress party enacted laws like RTF, MGNREGA, etc to distribute power to all the citizens of India. Therefore, we want #RahulGandhiWalaIndia i.e. #PowerfulIndia.

Our leader believes in the idea of a #DevelopedIndia in which the system of governance established by the congress party continuously works to resolve all the prevalent problems with the relevant solutions.

Under the leadership of Shri Rahul Gandhi, congress party enacted RTI Act and Lokayukta Act to address the grievance of corruption to make the system transparent. Therefore, we want #RahulGandhiWalaIndia i.e. #DevelopedIndia.

Secularism is an idea which means equal love for all the citizens of India despite of the differences in religious affiliation. Our leader strongly believes in the idea of Secularism. Congress party is completely devoted to work for all the citizens of India and is committed to remove all the prejudices and bias which is against the notion of a secular India. Therefore, we want #RahulGandhiWalaIndia i.e. #SecularIndia.

Rahul Gandhi wala India

#EducatedIndia

#IntelligentIndia

#PowerfulIndia

#DevelopedIndia

#SecularIndia

#CompassionateIndia

#CongresswalaIndia

#MyLeaderRahulGandhi

#RahulGandhi

10. How to survive the pressure of the battle, overcome all the challenges and win the desired competition.

14th Feb 2021

How to survive the pressure of the battle, overcome all the challenges and win the desired competition.

Survive the pressure of the battle

This is a huge, great and grand battle which the congress is fighting for survival. We should not surrender to this pressure but apply the equal force which should be six times in magnitude if not in quantity but in quality.

We must continuously try to encourage the citizens of India to get educated and get the real power of intelligence which will strengthen their minds to fight all the evils, prejudices and bias which some people are trying to infect their minds with. We are the creator of the largest democracy in the world and we are proud of the structure, system and the huge machinery which we have created for the sustenance of democracy which we have done for the benefit of the population of India. This system is the provider of all the amenities, facilities and infrastructure to enhance their state of living. They are an essential part of this system because it is the product of their hard work and intelligence. It is because of their participation that this system is created. They can innovate, create and improve this system. It is in their own interest to not ignore the continuous persistence of their forefathers to make this system of governance and they should further enhance this by contributing their ideas, innovations and notions. it is not advisable to destroy and remove this system entirely but to make it suitable according to the prevalent and contemporary demands. the infrastructure thus made to support the system is the result of 70 years of perseverance which has been possible due to mutual love, affection and devotion between congress and the citizens of India. There is an interaction of ideas between the congress party and the citizens of India which has resulted in the manifestation of this system which is done for the betterment of the people of India. therefore, we would request the citizens of India to continue this process of dialogue and discussion to further strengthen this system to take our country in the right direction of development and progress.

Overcome all the challenges

by continuously improving our strategy. we must have a comprehensive view of all the problems of India and must not concentrate our energies on the selected topics. there is a plethora of problem faced by our country being still at a developing stage. we must devise new ideas to make our country competitive with other developed countries. we must try to understand the expectations and concerns of the common man of India. In urban areas, youth is educated and expects the political parties to talk about issues related to infrastructure development, pollution mitigation, environmentally sustainable development, economic packages which would support their businesses, new schemes to be launched and new areas to be encouraged by the parties, etc. In rural areas, people need schemes which would enable them to sustain and support their livelihood, access to amenities and facilities which would make their lives smooth and easy.

there should be a discussion on ways we would increase the literacy in our country and give opportunities to the educated youth. there should be a discussion on the principles which congress party believes in like encouragement in scientific temper, importance of secularism, the relevance of socialist ideas in our country, inclusiveness which essentially means giving equal facilities to all the citizens while considering them equal, equality of opportunity, etc

win the desired competition

we must include the discussions on all the above-mentioned topics which would encompass the concerns of all the citizens of India. When the issues and problems of all the citizens are addressed we will win the competition. The strength of the congress party lies in all the citizens of India because we have been the provider and distributor of the power to the common man of India. Therefore, we must not feel threatened by this impermanent defeat.

11. Qualities of the machinery of governance

15th Feb 2021

The machinery for the system of governance is so beautifully crafted that it can never go against its own people. All the parts are created to serve their designed purpose that is to work for the welfare of the people of India and the staff recruited to execute and implement the decisions taken in the said direction. This machinery created is a result of intelligence of the citizens of India and is so designed that ant any fault found can also be corrected for the betterment of its functioning and to serve the intended purpose of development. Leaders may change and may make use of this machinery to achieve the purpose of development of India for it is the common aim of all the leaders who are chosen by the people. Therefore, we are grateful to the citizens of India and Congress party for such a flawless creation. We request them to continuously contribute to the system of governance with ideas and innovation to contribute to the welfare of the citizens and the development of India.

12. Relevance of the ideology of the grand old party

12th March 2021

Sir,

It is the responsibility of a leader to lessen the confusion in the minds of the children and youth of a country. From the variety of ideologies prevalent in the society to choose the most relevant one for the correct development of the thought process and to take our country on the right path of progress and development which will further translate in the correct actions and thoughts which will result into the permeation of truthful and honest ideas into all the levels of the society. Therefore, the correct ideology which includes the notions like secularism, socialism, scientific temper, freedom of expression, fearlessness, honesty and truthfulness, etc. should be encouraged to be understood by the young population to make these visible in their actions and thoughts. These are not only relevant because they have been practiced by the grand old party for years but also for their relevance in the present times as a solution of problems which are still prevalent i.e. poverty, illiteracy, malnutrition, undernutrition, casteism, religious intolerance, etc. which are mainly due to large population of our country. Therefore, this large population of our country which mainly constitutes of the young population need to be reared and nourished with good ideas and emotions and also provision should be made to nurture their families at least with the basic facilities so that they can get themselves educated and gain the intelligence which would result in the development of empowered citizens who are devoted to all the right values and virtues which are required for a better world.

13. My innovation about the ideals of Mahatma Gandhi

17th March 2021

Sir,

Let us remember, The Father of the Nation, Mahatma Gandhi and imagine the solution he would give to the youth of India in the present times in answer to the current problems faced by them. As I imagine, he would have explained the benefits of being educated. It is a process which an individual undergoes to gain the necessary information which would enable him/her to equip himself/herself with all the necessary tools to carve out a capable, intelligent and informed personality from the brain and physical body given to him/her by his parents. The strength thus gained by undergoing the explained process of getting educated empowers a personality to achieve all the possible options of achievements present in this world and also imagine the impossible and gain the strength to create the same. The resultant power when merges with the correct emotions and feelings of humanity, affection for all the living beings and devotion for the country will give you the power to attain all the right virtues and spread the correct message of love for humanity to the entire world which is the most important message and lesson given in all the religions. Therefore, in the present time, it is pertinent to say that Intelligence is equal to Godliness.

14. Message for the youth of India from the grand old party

18th March 2021

Sir,

You represent a major part of our population. You are the energy and strength of our country. From the year 1947 till today in which we gained independence, the congress party is known to make programmes and schemes to nurture this strength with all the facilities, amenities and opportunities. We have been creating institutions that are the temples of knowledge to nourish the intelligence which is bestowed on the youth of our country in abundance. This is done to channelise their energy in a creative direction and direct their intelligence for the attainment of excellence. We have always encouraged the environment of fearlessness to remove any prejudice or obstruction to prevent any hindrance on their path to attain all the virtuous achievements and correct beliefs for the welfare of our society. We don't support any kind of ideological confusion in the young minds which may divert their thought process to unfounded fears. Therefore, the congress party believes in the encouragement of scientific temper in the youth to empower them to have confidence in their education and excellence which would enable them to spread their knowledge to all the strata of Indian society and the feeling of humanity i.e. the devotion and affection for all despite of all the differences. The wisdom thereby gained will strengthen their minds to logically and rationally analyse their problems and they will be able to find the solutions of the same. The solutions thus obtained will remove the fears from their minds and restore their faith in humanity. The strength of all the population of a country is a force which is greater than any opposite force to the idea of a empowered and unified country. This strength is essential for the development of our country and the prosperity gained through the oneness of the purpose i.e. developed country will be unmatched, exemplary and unprecedented than any other country. Therefore, our country needs the ideological principles of congress like never before to guide and enlighten the minds of the young population.

15. What does it take to be an Indian Superhero

18th March 2021

Sir,

The Indian Superhero is seen as a personality who thinks for the benefit of all the strata of the society and fulfil the requirements of all according to their needs. He is a hero of the masses. He is seen as somebody who is sensitive to the problems of all the citizens of India. He is sufficiently intelligent to grasp the problem of the citizens and come out with the correct solutions of the same. For the last 70 years, he is known as somebody who wears white kurta pajama and works for the welfare of our country. He is affectionate towards the children of our country and a pillar of strength for the youth. He is inside the heart of every congressi. He can be compared to the Mr India of today who is dressed up in white kurta pajama. Therefore, "arrey karte hain hum pyaar Mr. India se, humko milna sau baar Mr. India se ".

Let us all make a pledge to follow all the right ideas and principles of Mr. White Kurta Pajama who has been with us for the past 70 years and empower the generation of today by explaining to them that it takes grit to wear that suit and fight against all the evils that disturb our nation. Therefore, to analyse "Does the man makes the suit or does the suit makes the man?". can be explained by saying that it takes courage to wear the white kurta pajama and fight for the welfare of the citizens and the courage that white kurta pajama gives makes a man capable of doing so.

Therefore, it will be our priority to make the youth of our country whether man or women to get encouraged to wear the white kurta pajama and get the power to do good for the country and prove our mettle to the entire world.

16. Rahul Gandhi is the most 'SUNDAR' politician of India.

21st March 2021

Rahul Gandhi is the most 'SUNDAR' politician of India. His 'SUNDARTA' lies in his efforts to maintain the dignity of his party and integrity of his party workers, the affection in his speech for the children and youth of our country, the devotion in his attitude for the culture of our country, the firmness he has for proving the correctness of the ideology of the Congress party, the determination with which he carries the legacy of his family and the intelligence with which he conducts the business of governance in our country. His 'SUNDARTA' lies in all of the above explained good points. The word 'SUNDAR' as epitomized by him is because of the unpretentiousness present in his character.

17. Intelligence is equal to godliness

22nd March 2021

Sir,

To develop and use your intelligence wisely is the correct way to pay reverence to the almighty who fondly created this human body equipped with brain and rendered intelligence to it to use the resources gifted by him and conduct the business of the many affairs in the world. Humans are the only species bestowed with the powers as we imagine to have been there in the god. As known in the Hindu scriptures to maintain the righteousness, to save the saints and to annihilate the wicked and the evil present in the society, God has manifested himself in the human body time and again. In today's world the business is conducted through the democracy in which the government is the regulatory body. People are the Mighty force which controls the ruler of the government according to their choice. Therefore it is the responsibility of the government to empower the people.

As we live in a modern world where a man is known by the achievement made by him and the wisdom gained by him, It is our duty to also strengthen the minds of the people by increasing good thoughts and ideas. In today's world it is important for us to realise that all the citizens are equally gifted by the God according to their capability. We are bestowed the intelligence in the quantity we can acquire by getting educated and according to the genetic. We must infuse our minds with good, thoughts, feelings and Ideas so as to make those reflect in our deeds. It is when our deeds mixed with good intentions give result according to our work, we gain the consequent power to be an achiever in the society. As the word power is synonymous with the quality of being godly and also as expected by the Indians to be, the power to do good gained by us makes us a true believer in the God and the right way to pay our reverence to the Mighty force which runs the entire Universe. Therefore each and every human who can conduct his work by making use of his Intelligence and according to the principles of humanity is sufficiently pious to prove that intelligence is equal to godliness.

18. Humanity is the real essence of Godliness.

23rd March 2021

Sir,

Humanity is the real essence of godliness. It is the most important lesson to be learnt from all the religious scriptures in the world. Therefore, the congress party urges the people of India to shed their unfounded fears and wear their true identity i.e. Indian, which is the source of confidence for all the Indians. It is our sincere request to all the citizens to strengthen their belief in the oneness of purpose i.e. Developed India and to have faith in the goodness of unity despite of all the differences. We are powerful because of the strength we gain through the feeling of affection and affinity we have for each other which conform to the sameness of character of every Indian and in agreement to the ideals of humanity which is the real identity of India. Therefore, we should make an effort to learn to protect ourselves from any influence which disregards the principle to give importance to humanity and work for the welfare of humankind or distance ourselves from having a humanitarian point of view of any situation or a problem. It is easy to be selfish but to think of the benefit of the entire world requires a big heart.

God is the biggest source of strength for the entire human race. He teaches us to have a feeling of affection for all. He is the mighty force that controls the entire universe. He puts life in the body of every living being. Therefore, as the owner of the entire universe he does justice by giving the same energy we call as life and to sustain it, the breath, to all the living organisms. Therefore, it is our duty to be respectful to all the life forms. It is our responsibility to protect and conserve all the life forms for the sustenance of life.

Humans are one of the best creations of the almighty. We have intelligence and the brain through which we conduct the business of the world. We must learn to respect the resources and the energy provided to us. We must devote our intelligence to the correct use of the same.

We are taught to not only desire and achieve the luxury present in the world but also to maintain the necessary balance between the different aspects of the environment. The environment which also includes the human aspect of the society. We should not pose a threat to the idea of humanity and should not endanger the necessary amity between the people of the world by unnecessary poaching of the correct ideologies which conserve the essence of humanity. Because love, affection and devotion to the cause of the humanity are the only saviours, next to god, to protect the life form called human race which he very fondly created.

19. How to predict, create and have a foresight for the bright future of our country

26th March 2021

Sir,

1. By letting go of the burden of the past events and happenings. The future is a new event and we must plan by shedding our inhibitions and prejudices of the past. We must not let our thoughts get disturbed by the negative emotions and memories of the past events. We must learn to create new memories by creating new events which must contribute to a positive future.

2. By inculcating positive feelings for creating the positive future happenings.

3. By creating positive thoughts for the innovation of the new strategy, encouraging the occurrence of the new ideas, giving a chance to the new leaders, infusing a new energy into the system to remove the inertia of staleness, etc.

4. The only thing that we need to carry from the past is the lesson of affection for the fellow citizens. The feelings of belongingness for our country by which we fasten ourselves to the roots of this country. The sense of responsibility to direct our work and thoughts for the development and progress of our country.

5. our vision for the country must include the programmes and schemes which should provide for the excellence of the youth and children of our country. We must encourage the sense of competition in the youth to achieve and excel in their respective fields for that would eventually result and add to the achievements of our country. We must encourage the innovations by the young in the system of governance also. We must accommodate their ideas and the way of working to encourage a new, modern and corruption-free system of governance free from all the vices and ill notions associated with the system of governance so that they can set a precedence for a transparent governance.

20. Introduction of the policy paper for 2024 elections for congress party. (as written by me)

4th May 2021

Sir,

Following is the introduction of the policy paper for the 2024 elections for the congress party as written by me. I request you to consider including the same in your manifesto and also take suggestions and opinions from the public.

Our Ideology

Key Points

1. Secularism

2. Socialism

3. Scientific Temper

4. Inclusive Development

5. Freedom of Expression

Necessity

For an all-inclusive development of India. Our idea of development gives importance to the human factor. Appropriate development of all the citizens of India will yield the correct status of prosperity and progress to India. Provision of all the basic amenities to the poor population of India will render capability to them to achieve and aspire. Fast-paced development with the latest technology will make India capable of competing with the rest of the world. By giving a chance to the native population of India to develop the latest technologies in India, the congress party will try to provide them with the opportunity to excel. We believe in the idea of inclusive development wherein all the citizens will be given all the amenities, facilities and opportunities to achieve the desired success. Congress party strongly believes in the idea to promote fearlessness in the actions and the thoughts of the citizens of India while encouraging the dissemination of the correct information. We believe in the idea of India where all the citizens are given equal opportunities for their growth without being subjected to any fear, prejudice and bias.

Relevance in the present time

We intend to channelise the energy of the youth of India to compete with the rest of the world while giving them all the required opportunities, amenities and facilities. We are devoted to encouraging all India's citizens to gain prosperity, literacy, intelligence, development, and progress. Thus, giving them the real power which would enable them to gain the strength to be self-sufficient.

Our vision for the bright future of India

India which is prepared for all the competitions, challenges and problems. India which is ready to excel, achieve and win. India which is powerful, self-sufficient and developed. It is the right time, we must be prepared to overcome all the challenges, achieve the capability of solving all the problems and win all the competitions. We must appreciate and encourage the youth of India who is desirous of achieving prosperity and power by working hard. We must include their voice in the process of governance and assure them of a bright future i.e. a self-sufficient and a powerful future for the India and a fearless and a developed future for its citizens.

21. necessity of the reliance on the congress party

23rd may 2021

Sir,

Congress Party's ideology includes the ideas like socialism, secularism, scientific temper, inclusive development, freedom of expression, etc. The people of India know that they can rely on the congress party in difficult times because they can rely on the above-mentioned principles. These principles are important because they empower the people by providing them all the necessary amenities, reduce the economic disparity, strengthen their thought process, create devotion to humanity and provide all the amenities, facilities, services and opportunities to all the citizens equally while considering them equal. It is a tendency of a human mind to rely on the goodness of thoughts and kindness in actions in difficult times for they can strengthen our heart and mind. Strength can only be derived from the resources which are unquestionably relevant and in plenty in nature. 99% of Indians believe in this goodness. Therefore, it is their tendency to rely on congress in difficult times. We must always try to propagate the thoughts and do the work that enriches other's experience with us. Congress party is committed to disseminate the right knowledge, do the just needs, practice the righteous path and uphold upright ideas.

22. A brief note about Mahatma Gandhi

26th May 2021

Sir,

Mohandas Karamchand Gandhi, famously known as Mahatma Gandhi in India and the entire world, is the epitome of bravery and courage. The grand image of Mahatma Gandhi is a result of his devotion to humanity. His principle of non-violence i.e. ahimsa as a tool to fight the atrocities waged against Indians by the Britishers is considered the most sought-after way to achieve justice. The intelligent execution of the same to the entire India lead to the achievement of the dream of 'Independent India'. His devotion to the establishment of truth and honesty in the acts and deeds of the Indians firmly established his status as 'Mahatma' in the hearts of Indians. He was devoted to his religion and expected the people of other religions to do the same. He wanted to establish Ram Rajya in the country which he defined as the governance in which all the citizens are entitled to get justice whether they are rich or poor. He dedicated his entire life to the accomplishment of one task i.e. Independent India. He relinquished all the wealth and money and lead a simple life. He became just like any other Indian of that time. He was an intelligent man and perseverance was one of his key strengths. Through his intelligence, he made a strategy to relieve the Indians from the atrocities of the Britishers and through his perseverance he could get that executed. He knew that to fight and overcome the fear generated in minds of Indians by the British forces we need to oppose them but not by causing any damage to human life but by the collective efforts of the Indians to stage ' Satyagraha' i.e. non-violent protests.

The innovation about the ideals of Mahatma Gandhi

In the present time, we can say that devotion to humanity and intelligence is the essence of godliness. We can show our devotion to God by applying both principles to our lives. Devotion to humanity i.e. to care about others in the way we care about ourselves and intelligence acquired through education empowers our mind to achieve the biggest aim we could desire. Collective human efforts to achieve a task is the biggest force in the entire world. Therefore, it is essential for the correct ideologies to guide us. The correct ideologies must include the ideals of humanity which essentially means to be devoted to the welfare of the entire humankind. To fight for the human values which encourages love for all. I appreciate the ideology of the Congress party for it is based on the points which encourage the welfare of all the citizens.

Intelligence developed by acquiring knowledge through education is the biggest investment one can make because that will yield not only all the comforts and wealth but also enriches our existence. One must try to include all the virtuous lessons in one's learning which means inculcation of noble thoughts and right values of which consideration for humanity is a must.

23. Happy Independence Day

14th August 2021

We cannot ignore and negate the contribution of the congress party in the infrastructure development. If we could now imagine being competent enough to be in the race of developed countries, it is because of the contribution of our party to the development of our country. We cannot let the lethargy of this impermanent defeat deter our spirits. It is our responsibility to encourage and appreciate the intelligence of our youth and we could do that only by making the infrastructure suitable, accessible and modern. Following are the areas in which we need to make huge improvements to make our country stand out in the global arena of development index.

Scientific innovation and technology development

This is the main area we need to infuse with new energy. We need to make programmes and introduce packages to encourage the involvement of the general public in the said sector. We know that we are intelligent, hard-working and capable to innovate in science. Therefore, we should not lag behind in appreciating and encouraging the talent of the youth who are interested in this field. Science is the future. Science is the way forward. We should make ways to support this intelligence in our own country. This is the real resource we can bank upon.

Education

To be able to achieve all the desired success one should be sufficiently educated. In this era of civilization, being educated is one of the greatest qualities one can acquire. If we could encourage the youth and children to attain the maximum of this quality we can ensure not only the prosperity of the citizen but also it will contribute to the development of the country.

Infrastructure development

We must encourage technology development in India with the help of its intelligent citizens for the fast-paced development of the infrastructure. We must ensure the use of the latest technologies to achieve the same.

Agriculture

We must ensure the easy availability of all the required tools, manures, seeds and irrigation facilities to the farmers for a better yield of agriculture.

Justice delivery system

No criminal should be spared from the punishment. We must ensure that the time of the public does not get wasted in the process to acquire justice which could have been contributing to the development of the nation.

Accessible Healthcare to the poor and rural population

We should accelerate this process so that no one gets deprived of this essential service.

Sustainable development

We cannot afford to play with the environment and not pay heed to the causes of its destruction. We should think of the future population while making use of any natural resource

Therefore, it is my sincere request to the top leadership of the congress party to consider the above-mentioned points as criteria for policy making for the manifesto of the elections. We Indians are wise enough to realise the importance of these points and we are aware of the development we can achieve by introducing the desired changes in the mentioned areas.

24. Idols of Indian democracy

21st August 2021

Sir,

Our party Congress, the pioneer in introducing the right changes in governance, is known to give several idols in Indian democracy. Indira Gandhi, who is known to introduce many right programmes through governance such green revolution, nationalisation of banks, etc is remembered as a lady who never surrendered to the conspiracies of the opponents and who never succumbed to the adversities of the circumstances. Our first prime minister, Pt. Jawahar Lal Nehru, who is known to introduce industrialization and the creation of the temples of knowledge in India is fondly remembered as a man who understood the wants and needs of the new country. The late prime minister of India Mr Rajiv Gandhi who is known to connect our country with technology always aimed to fulfil young India's aspirations. Our present leader Mr. Rahul Gandhi brought some wonderful laws which aimed at fulfilling Indians demands of transparency in the system of governance and empowering the common man through the provision of basic amenities to them.

We are bestowed with a rich legacy of work that we should not forget. Our party and its present leader deserve our support to continue the work done by our early party leaders. We must continue to devise new schemes, programmes and laws for the citizens of our country according to current demands and requirements. We as the grand old party of India is dutybound to provide all the amenities, facilities, services and infrastructure to the citizens of the country.

Though I am a minuscule part of this party I would like to see our party as a strong force that could deliver the above-mentioned promises. I would like to see our party emerge stronger after this impermanent defeat and to be ready to get the support of the people for a bright future of our country.